A Season of Prayer

40 Day

Devotional for Women

Written By

Nyreia Harrington-Stephens

Copyright © 2010 by Nyreia Harrington-Stephens

A Season of Prayer
by Nyreia Harrington-Stephens

Printed in the United States of America

ISBN 9781609572075

All rights reserved solely by the author. The author guarantees all contents are original and do not infringe upon the legal rights of any other person or work. No part of this book may be reproduced in any form without the permission of the author. The views expressed in this book are not necessarily those of the publisher.

Unless otherwise indicated, Bible quotations are taken from The New International Version of the Bible. Copyright © 1973, 1978, 1984 by Biblica.

www.xulonpress.com

Preface

I learned very early on in this journey called life that I am not an island unto myself. God in his infinite wisdom chose and ordained for me to live this life in community. The reality that comes with living in community is the blessing of living in unity with the Spirit of God. My life represents a small but significant part that is connected to a larger part which is the body of Christ. If you have spent any momentous time in the presence of the living God, he will begin to show you your part as he has done for me. Then you will begin to ask the Lord for your portion. I know now that my life is meant to be poured out like a drink offering. I present my body as a living sacrifice holy and acceptable unto Him for this is my reasonable service. The only way I can be poured out is if I drink the portion from the cup that the Lord has prepared for me. For those of you walking with the Lord, you know exactly what I mean. Will I dare not drink from the cup that the Lord has given me? The revelation and the epiphany is knowing that the drink is not meant for me, it is meant for others, those who are coming behind me and for those I am living in community with. For my life is not my own, it was bought with a price.

My journey has led me to connect with many wonderful people to whom I love deeply and adore. I thank God that I am not an island unto myself then my living would be in vain. To be effectual and fruitful in this life requires a connection to God and His people. There were times when the enemy desired to shift me as wheat, but those to whom I am in community with prayed for me. They prayed that when I was strengthened and encouraged that I would do the same for others, for this is the will of God for my life. So, this **Season of Prayer 40 Devotional for Women** is dedicated to all those who sowed into my life both from afar and near.

Dedications

To my husband Ronnie, for your unfailing encouragement and endearing love, I am forever grateful. Your contribution to my journey is one of poetic measure that without you my music would have no sound; it would only be clashing cymbals. Only Bible readers will get this one. Loving you has changed my life and receiving your love has been immeasurable. Only God knows the depth in which I speak.

To my 3 beautiful anointed daughters Jazmyne, Jhane', and Jaylynn, you each represent a part of my journey, I only pray that you would find the power and the significance in your individual pieces, it is truly a gift from God.

To my mom and my brothers, and extended family, you have been my rock and the solidarity needed to grow and spring forth in my calling in God.

To BTAW and Elect Lady, I honor you with the respect and honor you deserve. It is because of your YES to God, I was able to say YES. I am not sure if you fully knew how the power of your ministry of transformation would affect a once broken vessel like me, but I thank you for staying the course. **To my prayer warriors and FP team** thanks for staying on the front line. **To my NBC church family,** You Are............and More..

Love Nyreia

Contents

INTRODUCTION.. xiii

DAY 1 THE GOD WHO SEES....................................17
DAY 2 GOD HEARS YOU WHEN YOU CALL 19
DAY 3 GOD MY DELIVERER..................................21
DAY 4 INVITATION TO THE THIRSTY 23
DAY 5 ENTER INTO HIS REST 25
DAY 6 PUT ON THE FULL ARMOR OF GOD........27
DAY 7 POUR OUT YOUR SOUL UNTO THE LORD 29
DAY 8 TRUST IN THE LORD WITH ALL THY HEART..31
DAY 9 OPEN THE EYES OF MY HEART 33
DAY 10 TAKE HIS YOKE UPON YOU AND LEARN 35
DAY 11 ASK GOD FOR DIRECTION 37
DAY 12 MAKE GOD YOUR REFUGE 39
DAY 13 LET QUIETNESS BE YOUR STRENGTH..41
DAY 14 PRAYER & FASTING 43
DAY 15 REACH OUT AND TOUCH HIM..................45
DAY 16 TWO ARE BETTER THAN ONE..................47

DAY 17 SPEAK LIFE..49
DAY 18 IF YOU BELIEVE..51
DAY 19 THERE IS A TIME FOR
EVERYTHING 53
DAY 20 WAIT PATIENTLY UPON THE LORD 55
DAY 21 YET, SHALL I PRAISE HIM 57
DAY 22 I AM THE LORD'S SERVANT 59
DAY 23 MY HELP COMES FROM THE LORD 61
DAY 24 REJOICE IN OUR SUFFERINGS.................64
DAY 25 PRAY FOR THE COMFORTER 66
DAY 26 CAST DOWN IMAGINATIONS....................68
DAY 27 PRAY THAT YOUR FAITH FAILS NOT......70
DAY 28 GOD HAS NOT GIVEN YOU A SPIRIT
OF FEAR 72
DAY 29 PRAY FOR THE PILLAR..............................74
DAY 30 IN DUE SEASON 76
DAY 31 FIND JOY IN HIS PRESENCE......................78
DAY 32 I EXALT THEE OH LORD 80
DAY 33 PRAY FOR THE RENEWING OF
YOUR MIND 82
DAY 34 SUBMIT TO GOD AND RESIST
THE DEVIL 84
DAY 35 MEDITATE ON HIS WORD DAY AND
NIGHT..86
DAY 36 PRAY FOR THE PEACE OF GOD................89
DAY 37 PICK UP YOUR CROSS 91
DAY 38 WITH GOD ALL THINGS ARE
POSSIBLE...93

DAY 39 BE HIS WITNESS..95
DAY 40 FOR A SEASON 97

REFLECTION FROM THE AUTHOR 101
REFLECTION QUESTIONS...103

Introduction

John 14:6

Jesus answered, "I am the way and the truth and the life.
No one comes to the Father except through me.

The inspiration of this book **A Season of Prayer 40 day devotional for Women** was birthed out of my own wilderness experience. In the darkest and most painful times in my life, I reached out to God in heart wrenching prayer and soul searching devotion. I grabbed a hold of Him as Jacob did when he was in the wilderness and declared, "I will not let you go unto you bless me." My season of prayer ended with a fresh revelation of who God was in my life and who I was in Jesus Christ despite what I saw with my natural eyes. God begin to stir up in me, a desire to know him more and the power of His might. I will not lead you astray, God did not deliver me out of the season, He delivered me in the season of trouble. He taught me that the battle is not given to the swift but to those that endure to the end. Have you ever found yourself in a challenging season searching for direction but unable to find it? Those challenges could represent a season of mourning, depression, loneliness, exhaustion, separation, addiction, sickness, etc. You are desperately searching for the relief; joy, gladness, strength, encouragement, courage, healing, acceptance, etc. This 40 day season of prayer devotional will help catapult you into another dimension in Christ. Jesus said, "I am the way, the truth, and the life" (John 14:6). The beautiful thing about seasons is that they do change. You can appreciate the summer season of your life after you have endured the winter season of your life. No one ever tells you that some seasons require more of you spiritually, physically, emotionally, socially, and financially, and sometimes it is much more than you have to give. A season represents a period of time in your life marked by either glorious conditions or challenging conditions. Whatever season you find yourself in today, whether you are coming out of a challenging season or going into a challenging season, this 40 day season of prayer devotional for women will help you or someone you love endure that season with hope and encouragement. The Psalmist said, "Weeping may endure for a night, but joy cometh in the morning." (Psalm 30:5) That night the Psalmist speaks of could represent a challenging time in your life filled with adversity and a dim sense of self that pulls at the very core of your being. We are affirmed in this scripture that night will not last always, for morning will come and it reflects restoration and a renewed sense of self that accompanies the light. The interesting thing about my journey was that there were times that I didn't recognize that it was night. I felt like the wind had been knocked out of me and everything around me was dark. I was so distressed I had lost my sense of vision. I was down for the count. Mercy and grace got me up, and said to me, "You shall live and not die; you shall live to proclaim the salvation of the

Lord!" The biblical significance of 40 implies a period or time of testing, trial, probation, and it always ends with a period of restoration, renewal and revival. My life will be forever changed because I did not abort the season of testing and trials, but I allowed the Holy Spirit to birth a YES in my belly. That yes represented agreement with the will of the Father for my life. The gospel according to St. John tells us that in this life you shall have trouble, times of testing and tribulation, But be of good cheer, For our Lord has overcome the world (John 16:33). Allow God to show you his hessed love that is His steadfast love towards you, for you are the apple of His eye. My deliverance didn't come as I expected. I thought that I would wake up one day and the season would be changed. The season didn't change right away, but I had changed. I went into the season of testing and trials one person and came out another. If you think you will remain the same after having an encounter with the Living God, then maybe you should reconsider going on this 40 day journey. Maybe this isn't the season for you to embark on this journey to the High Places in God. But, if you feel the call of God to come up hither, I admonish you to behold the beauty of the Lamb. As you begin your 40 day season of prayer journey, embrace this season and find rest in the arms of His holiness. GO IN PEACE!

Day 1

"The God Who Sees"

Gen. 16:7-14
And the angel of the LORD found her by a fountain of water in the ***wilderness****....*
And she called the name of the LORD that spake unto her, ***Thou God seest me...***

Be affirmed today that whatever state or situation you find yourself in today, God sees you. God is not witnessing your life from afar; he is actually closer than you think. God will speak to you in the most darkest and distressful times in your life. Do not think that God is not aware of what is going on in your life. He is actually awaiting your invitation for him to be with you in your time of need. Most people attribute the evidence of God's awareness by what's going on in their lives and only if he removes them from that situation. Can you acknowledge His presence with you inside the storm? God is omnipresent! He can be with you while you are awaiting pending test results or while being present with someone else who hasn't seen their wayward child in days. God saw Hagar in the wilderness; she was surprised to find that God met her in the wilderness. Will you proclaim as she did, Thou God seest me?

Prayer

Dear Heavenly Father,
Help me to know that you are with me today.
I thank you that
You are a God who sees. I pray that I will learn
to embrace this spiritual truth
daily and may I help others to know that you see
and that you care.
I pray that you will meet me in the midst of my
circumstances today, I invite you in.
I thank you that there is no where that I can hide
from you, because you are omnipresent.
I acknowledge my insufficiency and I lay hold to your all
sufficiency. For you are the God who sees and knows
all about me.

In Jesus Name, Amen

Day 2

"God Hears You When You Call"

Psalms 5:1-2
Give ear to my words, O LORD, Consider my meditation.
***Give heed to the voice of my cry*.....**

Before you pick up the phone to call a friend today, will you consider calling on God instead? Life is filled with difficult days. Some days are better than others and we often want to share those days with someone. Especially, when we are facing a trial or experiencing some form of persecution. Even on occasions when you want to share an unexpected blessing that has come your way. God longs to hear from you whatever the news is. He hears you when you call. That call can come in the form of a praise, worship, meditation, and prayer. God is a better listener than most people think he is. Calling on God promotes intimacy with him and nurtures your fellowship with the Father. When we share our lives with God we actually bring him joy. In this act of humble submission, we call on the Lord acknowledging his ability to reveal himself to us as our Heavenly Father. Therefore, we cry Abba Father.

Prayer

Abba Father,
I call on your holy name today, acknowledging your supremacy in the Earth.
You are the good shepherd, and your sheep know your voice. Lord, here my cry for mercy
and grace today. Lead me beside the still waters, and restore my soul. I lay at your alter all those things that concern me today. I know that you hear me, and I trust in your love for me. Fill those desolate places within me with the abundance of your Spirit. May I increase in wisdom and strength today. Give me power from on high to tread upon the adversary. As a young daughter calls for her father when she is in need, I call on you my Heavenly Father to supply all of my needs according to your riches and glory.

In Jesus Name,
Amen

Day 3

"God My Deliverer"

Psalm 50:15
And call upon me in the day of trouble;
***I will deliver you**, and you will honor me…..*

Have you ever felt like you were drowning in the lake of adversity, temptation, unfavorable circumstances, a marriage in trouble, a child who refuses to be obedient, and a job that never acknowledges your worth? The day of trouble in this passage expresses the sentiment of those days when you desire to be set free from life's challenges that seek to overtake you. Sometimes the situation or circumstance must go through its process before the matter is resolved. But, the Lord your God can deliver you by giving you peace of mind or by being a very present help in that matter. Deliverance can come in many forms. Deliverance can be God giving you strength for the battle ahead. It could also look like fresh revelation of God as your deliverer. The saving power and strength of God is exhibited in our weakness. This is the time when it is not good to lean onto your own understanding, but to acknowledge God in all of your ways, and he shall direct your path. The prescription or the recipe for deliverance is tailored made for your situation by the Great Physician, will you trust his prognosis?

Prayer

Dear Lord, I stretch my hands to thee, no other help have I known. My view of my life's circumstances may be shallow and dim, but Lord your vision is deep and bright. In the day of trouble, I will call on your name because you are my deliver in whom I trust. Today, I choose to trust in your authority in my life as Father. Your love alone God provides hope and solace. You called the end from the beginning, you know the way that I must go, and when I have been tried, I shall come forth as pure gold. May I trust the process of my deliverance. It is in you that I live, move and have my being. As I pursue holiness today, continue to weed out those thoughts that try to hold me captive. I will cast down every imagination and every high thing that seeks to exalt itself against the knowledge of Christ in my life today.

In Jesus Name,
Amen

Day 4

"Invitation to the Thirsty"

Isaiah 55: 1
*"**Come, all you who are thirsty,***
***come to the waters**; and you who have no money,*
come, buy and eat!

Whenever there is a sense of deep longing or uneasiness in your spirit and soul, this could signify that you are thirsty. There are seasons in our lives where we need our Heavenly Father to lead us and guide us beside the still waters so that we can drink. This thirst signifies a need to be filled up with living waters. Consider the source of where you go to quench your thirst. If we try to quench this thirst by not allowing Jesus Christ to meet us at the well, we could go away still thirsty. If you drink the water that Christ desires to give you, you will never thirst again. Worship opens the spring of water to which your spirit and your soul will experience the overflow of the Master's presence. The invitation to the thirsty is an invitation into the presence of the Almighty. There is an exchange that takes place when we worship God in spirit and in truth. His Spirit then begins to pour into our spirit everlasting life which is the ever-present thirst quencher. Stay in His presence then you will overcome your thirst. Ask the Lord to anoint your head with oil today, so that your cup can runneth over.

Prayer

Dear Heavenly Father,

As the deer pants for the water, so does my soul thirst for you. May a well spring up inside of me today that causes my entire being to know the hope of glory. I am seeking you today Lord, while it is early and while you may be found. Father, you said in your word that as long as the earth remains, there will always be seedtime and harvest. As I sow my seeds of worship to you today, may I receive an abundance of your Spirit to fulfill every dry place within me. For in your presence is fullness of joy, and there is no lack in you. I came today desiring more of your presence, but when I leave your presence shall go with me. I accept your invitation to the waters; please accept my offering of worship. I worship you for who you are the Alpha and the Omega, my soon coming king.

In Jesus Name,

Amen

Day 5

"Enter into His Rest"

Hebrews 4:1

*Therefore, since the promise of **entering his rest** still stands, let us be careful that none of you be found to have fallen short of it.*

The bible encourages us not to grow weary in our well doing along this journey called life, for if we faint not He shall renew our strength. The incentive that God denotes here is that growing weary or being worn-out is not His perfect will for our lives, so we should consider his promise to us. Our lives can become overwhelming and distressful, if we allow them to. If we find ourselves with a lack of peace or very short tempered with our love ones, then we should take a moment and discern how this is affecting our spiritual and physical health. This could signify that it is time to rest and retreat. The promise of God still stands; we are encouraged to enter His rest. Entering the rest of God promotes self care, self-awareness, solitude, and soul searching. When we dwell in the secret place of the Most High, then we will find rest for our souls. God's promises to us are always yes and amen. He will cover you and become a safe place for you and restore your soul. We must be careful not to enter into his rest and fall short of the grace that God has provided us. On the seventh day after creation and God had finished the work He performed, God rested. How is God calling you to honor the Sabbath today?

Prayer

Master,
I glorify your holy name today and honor you with the fruit of my lips. You are good and your mercy endures forever. Open my eyes to see when you are calling me to enter into your rest. May I not resist the prompting of the Holy Spirit. God, you created my innermost being, you knew me before I was in my mother's womb, you know my limits, help me to discern them. I desire truth in my inner most being. Lord, I do not want my labor to be in vain, unless you keep me Lord it will all be for naught.
I will not fall short of entering into your rest today.

In Jesus Name,
Amen

Day 6

"Put on the Full Armor of God"

Ephesians 6: 10-13
Finally, be strong in the Lord and in his mighty power...
***Therefore put on the full armor of God**, so that when the day of evil comes, you may be able to stand your ground, and after you have done everything, to stand.....*

Today you will arise and dress yourself appropriately for whatever you need to accomplish today. When you are getting dressed, you have to make sure you are dressed appropriately for the season. If it is winter you want to make sure that you dress for the aggressively cold climate. If it is summer, you want to make sure that you don't over exert yourself by dressing in too many layers. Whatever season you find yourself in spiritually, you need to make sure you are dressed appropriately. We are encouraged on how to dress by God's word and that is to put on the full armor of God. Putting on the armor of God requires acknowledgment that we need to be strong in the Lord and in his mighty power and not our own. Being alert and being prepared can offset the plans of the enemy in your life today and expose and extinguish his attacks. This is not something we can do with our carnal minds, for our carnal minds are insufficient. We need revelation knowledge and insight into the plans of the enemy of our souls so that they can be spoiled. If I take an umbrella with me when it is expected to rain, I won't get wet because I have prepared for the climate. If I dress in the full armor of God daily, I will not be ignorant of the devices of the evil one, and I can stand my ground in my Lord's protection.

Prayer

Jehovah Nissi,
I petition your throne today Lord, so that I may know you today as Jehovah Nissi, my banner and my shield. Today, I dress myself appropriately to battle unseen spiritual forces that would try to lead me down the wrong path. I will pray in the Spirit today in all occasions, using my shield of faith, my belt of truth which is in Christ Jesus, my sword which represents your word concerning my life. I will also use my helmet of salvation that assures me of my victory. I am the righteousness of God. You shall plant my feet today on a path of peace. Having done all I can do, I will stand and see the salvation of the Lord.

In Jesus Name, Amen

Day 7

"Pour Out Your Soul unto the Lord"

I Samuel 1: 15
And Hannah answered and said...
I am a woman of a sorrowful spirit:
but have poured out my soul before the LORD.

When a glass or container becomes full to the point where the contents could spill over, this would indicate that you need to pour some of the contents out to prevent a possible mess that you or someone will need to clean up. This is a natural illustration of a greater spiritual revelation of how there are times in our lives when we get full of the contents or situations of life. Hannah acknowledged that she was a woman who had begun to be overfilled with stressful situations or unexpected matters. Hannah began to pour out her soul unto the Lord. Essentially, she began to release anxiety, fear, nervousness, stress, worry, doubt and unbelief unto her God. There will come a time in your life when you will need to let go of the things in your life or be overtaken by them. If you don't pour them out before the Lord, you could be left with a mess for you or someone else to clean up. Deep calls out to deep. Pouring out your soul unto God means that you recognize that if you don't seek his face and not his hand, you might not make it to the next level in Him. A beautiful woman is a woman who does not wear her life like a mere piece of her wardrobe, but one who gives her life to the one who gave her life. This may cause you to pray out of your place of pain or brokenness, and ask God to grant you favor. After you have poured out of your distress, ask God to refill you with his peace.

Prayer

Almighty God, I pray for a divine release in my life today and in the lives of my loved ones. I sit at your feet and I open up my alabaster box, and I pour out my soul unto you. I cry out to the living God, that you will grant me favor in my time of need. Remember me today, as you remembered Hannah, bless me indeed and enlarge my territory. Expand my place of ministry to you today and my soul will magnify you, Oh Lord! I have searched the Heavens high and the Earth below, and I have found none like you. Mold me and shape me so that I may understand that I have been chosen for such a time as this.

In Jesus Name, Amen

Day 8

"Trust in the Lord with all thy Heart"

Proverbs 3:5-6
Trust in the LORD with all your heart *and lean not on your own understanding;*
in all your ways acknowledge him,
and he will make your paths straight.

Out of the heart flows the issues of life. There are events, times and seasons in your life where you are not going to understand what God is doing. You may wonder if God has totally abandoned you to wrestle for yourself. We must begin to deal with the issues that infringe upon our lives, so that are hearts are not overtaken by adversity. The beauty of surrender means that we have come to a place in our journey with the Lord, that we have begun to trust in the Lord with all of our heart. The struggle to this place of surrender takes a great leap of faith and a metamorphous of inner self. If we are not careful, our hearts will devise many plans, not understanding that it is only the purposes of God that prevail. Acknowledge God's purposes for whatever season you are in today. He knows the way out, you must trust in His divine plan for your life. His plan towards you is good and not evil, His plans is to give you an expected great end. His thoughts are higher than your thoughts, his ways, are higher than your ways. He will make the crooked places straight. Broad is the way that leads to destruction, narrow is the way that leads to the abundant life, few take this way. Will you trust in the Lord today?

Prayer

Wonderful Counselor, Great I Am,
I give you high praise today! Create in me a clean heart; renew in me the right spirit. May your purposes prevail in my life today. You are not a man that you should lie; watch over your word to perform it. I trust you with every area of my life today, even those areas that I feel the most vulnerable in. Your ways may challenge me, and it may be narrow, make my path straight. I reject the broad and easy path that leads to destruction. Help me to discern the two. I surrender all unto thee. Prepare me as your bride, without spot or wrinkle. Keep me from falling and present me before your glorious presence. I will not wander in the wilderness when you have given me the way of escape.

In Jesus Name, Amen

Day 9

"Open the Eyes of My Heart"

Ephesians 1:18
Pray that the eyes of your heart may be enlightened
in order that you may know the hope to which he has called you...

When crossing the intersection of a busy street, you must have your eyes open and look in the direction to which you are going. If your eyes are closed you may not see that car that is coming your way. The benefits of having your eyes open is that you will see the car coming and halt and avoid the accident. Pray that the eyes of your heart are opened so that you can see what your Heavenly Father has destined for your life. If the eyes of your heart are closed, you will not know the hope to which he has called you. God speaks to our hearts and not to our intellect. Especially if you are in a dark season in your life, you will need the Lord to shine light upon your path. God will be a pillar of cloud by day, and a pillar of fire by night. It is He who has called you out of the darkness into His marvelous light. God's word is a lamp unto your feet, and a light unto your path. As you stand at the crossroads today, ask for the ancient path, the proven paths. Stand! Watch! Hear! See what he may show you. Go in His way everlasting. God desires to take you from glory to glory, strength to strength, but you must have the eyes of your heart open to receive the Master's touch.

Prayer

Dear Heavenly Father.

I want to see you today! Open the eyes of my heart Lord so that I know beyond measure the hope of your calling upon my life. I will look with my spiritual eyes upwards towards your place of dwelling, from which cometh my help, my way out of darkness cometh from you. Lead me in your path everlasting. I will not look back when you have told me to look ahead and press towards the mark of my high calling in Christ Jesus. I shall run the race that has been set before me. Speak to my heart today that I may know you more. I love you God and I desire to walk with you daily. For I am a friend of God!

In Jesus Name, Amen

Day 10

"Take His Yoke upon You and Learn"

Matthew 11:28-30
Take my yoke upon you and learn ... *For my yoke is easy and my burden is light......*

God has equipped and prepared you for every good work. That work includes all that he has called you to do such as: care for yourself and your family, good works of service in the house of God, minister to those he has placed in your path, etc. God's burden is light and His yoke is easy. If you find yourself heavily burdened today, begin to cast off restraints. Take His yoke upon you and learn of Him. His burden is light and his yoke is easy. Learn today that He is a rewarder of those who diligently seek Him. This is the day that the Lord has made, you should rejoice and be glad in it. He is our burden bearer, he is our Elohim. He is the God of Israel who led the Israelites 40 days in the wilderness and their shoes did not wear out. He provided for them daily. Worry produces the yoke; dependence on God destroys the yoke. Will you allow God to be your Elohim? Will you take His yoke upon you and learn of His proven faithfulness to his children? Ask God to reveal to you today anything that you may be carrying that he has not ordained for you to carry. Ask God for courage to lay down those things that the Holy Spirit reveals. Discern the season of your life in regards to your commitments. Allow the Lord to instruct you in your way of obligations. The divine will of God is for you to have yoke that is easy and burden that is light. Ask Him to show you His perfect will for your life. Write down the revelation, for it awaits an appointed season in your life, though it is delayed wait for it. He will give you the desires of your heart.

Prayer

Jehovah Shalom,

God you are my peace today! I pray that you would remove anything in my life that seeks to burden me and steal my peace. My desire is to please you Father. May I observe your statues today and remember my oath to you, to love the Lord my God, with all of my heart, my mind, and my soul. Destroy every yoke and remove every burden by releasing your anointing into my life. I live to praise you! You are the Potter and I am the clay. As the clay is in the Potter's hand, so is my life in your hands. At the end of my life, I want to hear you say to me, well done my faithful daughter, enter into my rest!

In Jesus Name, Amen

Day 11

"Ask God for Direction"

Jeremiah 6:16
This is what the LORD says:
"Stand at the crossroads and look; ***ask*** *for the ancient paths,* ***ask*** *where the good way is, and walk in it, and you will find rest for your souls.....*

Having a teachable spirit is very important in order to find yourself in the center of God's will. There will come a time in your life where you will need some godly direction concerning your life and the decisions you need to make? You may need direction concerning possible health treatments, family and relationship decisions, career moves, etc... Maybe you think you know exactly which direction you are to go in? God's ways are often totally different than ours, be willing to be taught to always look for His ways. We are always to seek the Lord for His direction. The direction that he has for His children to go in is often in the direction of the storm and not away from the storm. The natural instinct is to run in the opposite way of our adversities, and not to stand and face them in the strength of the Lord. King David stood in the face of the giant, and in the strength of the Lord. Many around him had run from the giant, running from obstacles in the form of giants only keep you bound and in a restless state. God knows the way that we should go in and when you have been tried you will come out as pure gold. Stand at the crossroads today in whatever decision you need to make, ask the Lord to show you the way that is good and profitable for your victory in Him. Allow His leading to turn a restless situation into a place of rest for your soul. He will lead you beside the still waters and restore you. Ask and it shall be given unto you.

Prayer

Dear Father,
I extol your name today, for you are good and your mercy endures forever.
When I find myself needing to know what path you would have me to go in today, may I seek you first and your Kingdom that all things may be added unto me. You are the Good Shepherd, and I shall not be in want. Lead me today beside the still waters, so that I may hear you when you speak to me. I am asking for direction and instructions today, so that I may live a life that is pleasing unto you. I look towards the hills from whence cometh my help, my help cometh from you O'Lord!

In Jesus Name, Amen

Day 12

"Make God Your Refuge"

Psalm 91:1-2
He who dwells in the shelter of the Most High will rest in the shadow of the Almighty.
I will say of the LORD,
*"**He is my refuge** and my fortress, my God, in whom I trust."*

It is common to look for shelter in the midst of a storm. There are different storms that surface from time to time, such as thunderstorms, tornadoes, and even hurricanes. There are storms in our personal lives that surface such as an unexpected illness, divorce or separation, sudden death of a loved one, depression or anxiety attacks. When a storm hits you do not want to be caught out in the storm alone. You want you and your loved ones to be found somewhere safe. God's word tells us that in this life we will have trials, sometimes these trials can be interpreted as storms. The Lord longs for us to choose His holy habitation as our refuge. Will you make God your refuge today? There is shelter and rest in the secret place of the Most High. It is in His divine protection that you will find rest. After the storm has ceased you can be assure that God still desires your fellowship. Seek the Lord while he may be found. He will send the Comforter to you in the midst of the storm. He will give His angels charge over you so that you will not dash your foot against a stone in the midst of the trial. Will you receive the Lord's invitation to dwell with Him, in the shadow of the Almighty?

Prayer

Jehovah Nissi,
You are my banner and my shield. I glorify your holy name today. I seek you today with my whole heart. I am not afraid of the terror by night or the pestilence that stalks by midday, for in you Lord do I trust. A thousand shall fall at my side, ten thousand at my right, but none shall come nigh my dwelling. It is in you that I live, move and have my being. Though the storms of life rage, one thing will I be sure of, and that is the security of your word, that I will dwell in the house of the Lord forever that I may inquire in your temple. Draw nigh to me Father as I draw nigh to you. Search my heart Lord, and when you find anything that is not like you, I ask you to remove it. I accept your invitation to make you my refuge in the day of trouble.

In Jesus Name,
Amen

Day 13

"Let Quietness Be your Strength"

Isaiah 30:15
This is what the Sovereign LORD, the Holy One of Israel, says:
in quietness and trust is your strength.......

Those that train for the Olympics and other physical activities, have to make sure that they have built up their endurance. The endurance needed to sustain the strenuous amount of energy needed to complete their goal. Those that participate in marathons often do not speak while they are running because when they talk they are releasing energy that is needed to reach the finish line. There will be seasons in your life, where you will need to endure and obtain the needed strength to obtain the prize of victory over life's circumstances. The Apostle Paul teaches us to run the race that is set before us, likening the Christian journey to that of a marathon. God may be requiring you to hold your peace during this season in your life. In quietness and trust will be your strength. Do not grow weary or exhausted in your well doing by speaking things that are not the Father's will. Life and death is in the power of the tongue. The race is not given to the swift but to those that endure to the end. The Bible records that as Jesus was on His way to the cross, He was oppressed and afflicted, yet he did not open his mouth; he was led like a lamb to the slaughter, and as a sheep before her shearers is silent, so he did not open his mouth. Being quiet in the midst of a difficult season requires the discipline of self-control. Our weakness and quietness is made perfect in His strength.

Prayer

Dear Lord,
I trust you. You are the Lover of my soul.
My soul doth magnify the Lord!
You are a very present help. No weapon that is forged against me shall prosper, nor shall any tongue that should rise against me, for you Lord will condemn. May I say only what I hear you say. In quietness and confidence shall be my strength. I pray that you will grant me endurance, perseverance, and peace of mind today. For you require a broken heart, and a broken and contrite spirit, these you will not despise. May my conversation today be chaste and coupled with fear. A meek and quiet spirit is my desire for I live to please you.

In Jesus Name,
Amen

Day 14

"Prayer & Fasting"

Mark 9:29
And he said unto them,
This kind can come forth by nothing, ***but by prayer and fasting****.*

When seasons of change come sometimes the circumstances are not always favorable. The human nature tends to resist change because the old ways are comfortable and familiar. No one wants to be uncomfortable enough to see God bring you forth out of the miry clay of despair and destruction into a season of harvest and plenty. Moving forward in God will cause you to leave something's, some people, and some ways behind. There are something's that God wants to remove from you, and it will require prayer and fasting. Prayer will help prepare your heart for the ability to fast (resist) that very thing that God wants to purge from your life. The Lord knows what's ahead, you must trust his leading! Look at the trees when the fall season comes, they often lose their leaves before the snow arrives. God does not leave the trees bare; it's only for a season. God will not leave you bare or alone, it's only for a season! When spring arrives (the new season), the trees begin to bloom again, new leaves spring forth. God is doing a new thing in your life today, do you not perceive it? Come forth today into your destiny and the awareness of who you are in Christ, prayer and fasting precedes your next breakthrough. Walk into your new season with joy and expectation!

Prayer

Lord,

I trust you today. Show me those things that you want me to lay down, that I may follow after you in spirit and in truth. I seek you with my whole heart and mind and soul. I am praying because I desire to know your perfect will for my life. As you lead me I will fast so that those things that are not like you I will willingly release. I thank you that no weapon that is forged against me shall prosper. I thank you that old things have passed away and behold new things shall remain because you love me and I am called according to your purpose.

In Jesus Name,
Amen

Day 15

"Reach Out and Touch Him"

Mark 5:25-34
When she heard about Jesus, she came up behind him in the crowd ***and touched his cloak,***
Because she thought, if ***I just touch his clothes,*** *I will be healed.......*

Adversity has a way of bringing many to a place of being stuck and confused. When unexpected circumstances and emotional or physical pain comes it will try to cause you to stop seeking God for your healing, for your deliverance, and for your peace. You will need to participate in your deliverance! God's will is that you prosper, be in good health and that your soul prospers. God has not brought you to this place so that you will die and stop living life here. You shall live and not die! You will need to reach out and grab hold of your Heavenly Father's word concerning your life. Speak life over your circumstances today. Faith without works is dead.

When a check is deposited into your bank account, you must go and withdraw that money if you want to use it. God has made deposits into your heavenly bank account and he is awaiting you to make as many withdrawals as you need and use it. God will give the Holy Spirit to those that ask him. Ask God for His Holy Spirit to dwell within you today. Reach out to those God has placed in your life to be of support and encouragement. God works through community.

Embrace the process, trust his leading, and touch him today in your worship of who he is in your life.

Prayer

God,

Today was not promised nor was yesterday. Yet, you woke me up this morning and I am thankful that you did not forsake me. I am releasing those things in my life that have prevented me from fully trusting you.

I shall participate in my own deliverance! Sin is no longer my master, I will no longer be held captive by anything except your love. I reach out to you today in spirit and in truth. Father, use what the devil meant for evil and turn it around for my good. I receive my deliverance today, and I shall live and not die to receive the blessings of God for my life. Lord, arrest the evil one and terminate his attacks against me today. I will resist the enemy and he has to flee. Healing waters flow from Heaven and penetrate my mind, for I have the mind of Christ. I am the redeemed of the Lord and it is so!

In Jesus Name,

Amen

Day 16

"Two are Better than One"

Ecclesiastes 4: 9-10
Two are better than one, *because they have a good return for their work:*
If one falls down, his friend can help him up…

Life has a way of throwing unfavorable circumstances in your direction. But God has assured us that we are not without hope or help. Often times life circumstances can knock the wind out of you. When you experience hard times and what seems like irreparable damage to your heart or self esteem, God often sends someone who he has appointed and anointed to speak a word of hope and encouragement to you. Life is not meant to be lived alone, two are better than one; there will be times in your life when you will need a lift. The awesomeness of God is that the one he sends to lift you up could be the one you least expect. Jesus sent the disciples out in two's because two are better than one. There is safety in the multitude of counselors. When you are down in spirit, you will need to reach up to Heaven so that you can be lifted up. Pride comes before a mighty fall. During times of distress do not let pride or envy cause you to fall deeper into depression or oppression or even sadness. Humble yourself under the mighty hand of God, that he might exalt and lift you up in due season. Weeping may endure for a night but joy cometh in the morning. Look up when you are down, to the hills from which cometh your help, your help cometh from the Lord. That help may come in the form of a friend.

Prayer

My Father which Art in Heaven, I praise you today for you are my Redeemer, in you do I trust. I know that you have a plan for my life today, and that plan is to help me and not to hurt me. Search me Lord know my heart. If you find anything that is not like you, I ask that you remove it. I will not fret over evildoers, for they shall soon be cut down. The steps of the righteous are ordered by God and I am the righteousness of God! Though I might fall under unfavorable circumstances today, I shall not be utterly cast down for you O' LORD will uphold me with your hand. If you send a friend to help me, I will remember that two are better than one.

In Jesus Name,
Amen

Day 17

"Speak Life"

Proverbs 18:21
The tongue has the power of life and death, *and those who love it will eat its fruit.*

When you find yourself in a season of testing and trials, you must be careful what you are speaking. Your tongue can set into motion more testing and more trials. Examine yourself today, what are you speaking? During times of distress, it is very hard not to speak negatively. It will take self-discipline and assurance of the knowledge of God's word that says the tongue has the power of life and death. Make a conscious decision today, will you speak life or will you speak death? Some things that have died were supposed to die, but there were something's (relationships, health, finances, etc.) that many have killed with the very words from their own mouth. Yes, it does matter what is coming out of your mouth, you can build up or tear down. If you have been speaking death to a situation, you can repent today and begin to make confessions of life over you and your loved ones. If a loved one or a present situation disappoints you and you want to proclaim death over it, you will need to halt. That means hold up, access the situation, look and listen, and take authority over your mouth. If you want to see dead things in your life be resurrected, you must speak life! Speak life over your relationship with God, speak life over your health, speak life over your mind and your finances today, do not be deceived whatsoever a man sows, he shall reap. There is a way of speaking that seems right unto a person, but in the end there is destruction. The straight and narrow path of speaking leads to life for it is birthed out of obedience to God. Jesus told Lazarath to arise and come forth from the grave, what is God leading you to call forth in this season of your life?

Prayer

Almighty God,
All Glory and Honor is ascribed unto you! For you are good and your mercy endures forever. I choose to speak life today, no matter what situation or what circumstances I find myself in. I am blessed in the city; I am blessed in the field. I am blessed when I come out and when I go in. My family is blessed; no weapon that is forged against me shall prosper. Grant me supernatural favor so that I may continue to run this race that has been set before me. I am the head and not the tail. I am whole in you Father, nothing missing, nothing broken. I am prosperous; everywhere that I step today is blessed. I cancel every assignment of the enemy that has been waged against me today. I will not grow weary in my well doing, for soon I shall reap a harvest of the word of God that I have chose to speak over my life.

In Jesus Name,
Amen

Day 18

"If you Believe"

Matthew 21:21-22

*Jesus replied, "I tell you the truth, **if you have faith and do not doubt**, you can say to this mountain, 'Go, throw yourself into the sea,' and it will be done.*
***If you believe**, you will receive whatever you ask for in prayer"…….*

Are you living in an uncertain season today? Do you question whether or not you will survive or recover? These questions often plaque both the believer in Christ and the non-believer. Life is filled with swift transitions. In this season your life may be changing, relationships may be changing, and you are facing a mountain of pain, hurt, rejection and financial ruin. This is when you must begin to speak to the mountains in your life, and declare you shall overcome. Pray to the Lord of the Harvest today, and believe and speak. Speak restitution to your finances; tell debt that you break your agreement with poverty today. Speak restoration to your mind and spirit; tell the pain of un-forgiveness that you choose to release bitterness and resentment and they must go! Your ability to stand in the face of adversity requires faith. You must believe that God is a rewarder of those who diligently seek Him. Also, that you have been given power from on high to trample over the adversity in your life through your faith. You must decrease so that your Heavenly Father can increase in you. He will give you beauty for ashes, and the oil of joy for mourning, believe and receive from the Master's hand today. Maybe you're struggling in your faith today and you have some doubts about how God will bring you out of this season, declare to your Lord, "Lord, I believe but help my unbelief."

Prayer

Lord,

I love you Lord and I accept and embrace your love for me. Encourage me in your word today. I'm struggling to stay in faith in the midst of heart ache and suffering. I believe in you and I believe you can heal and deliver me in this season. I chose not to allow doubt and fear to have dominion in my life. I am more than a conquer; greater is he that is in me than he that is in this world. I speak to anything that would block or hinder me from experiencing full communion with you and I command it to be dismantled now. I confess with my mouth and I believe in my heart that Jesus is the Son of God. Jesus is my Savior and he shall save me from my enemies today. Lord, I believe, help my unbelief.

In Jesus Name,
Amen

Day 19

"There is a Time for Everything"

Ecclesiastes 3: 1
There is a time for everything, *and a season for every activity under heaven*

You are the handiwork of God. You were fashioned in the image of your maker at the appointed time of your birth. There is a time for everything, and a season for every activity under heaven. Whatever time or season you find yourself in today, be encouraged! There is a time to weep, if it is your season to weep, weep with a purpose knowing that He who is calling you out of darkness is faithful and just to keep you during this season. If it is your season to mourn, mourn and be comforted by his presence. If this is your time to be silent, let quietness and confidence be your strength. The Bible tells us to discern the times. You must acknowledge this time in your life, so that you will not forget who is keeping you. Remember it is the LORD your God that is leading you along the way in this season, these forty days, to humble you and to test you in order to know what is in your heart, whether or not you will keep his commands. To teach you that you cannot live on bread alone but on every word that comes from the mouth of the LORD. Hold on to the profession of your faith until the chronos (chronological) time meets up with your kairos (appointed time) of deliverance. Remain faithful and obedient until the word of the Lord proves you true. Don't rush this time and always remember, Jesus, full of the Holy Spirit, was led by the Spirit in the desert, where for forty days he was tempted by the devil. When the devil has finished all this tempting, he will leave you until an opportune time.

Prayer

My Redeemer,
Thank you for redeeming my life from the evil one. I thank you that my hope is in you alone. During this time and season of testing, I will remain faithful and obedient. Lord, help me to grow and mature in this season so that I may bear fruit in my due season. I am like the tree that is planted by the rivers of living water, my leaves will not wither and whatever I do in your name I shall prosper in. Holy Spirit, help me to hold out until my season of change comes. I know that you give strength to the weary, and I am a hearer and a doer of your word. Lord, birth out your purposes in my life during this season. Teach my fingers to war, and may I not abort this season, but endure as a good soldier of the Lord.

In Jesus Name,
Amen

Day 20

"Wait Patiently upon the Lord"

Psalm 40:1-2

I waited patiently for the LORD*; he turned to me and heard my cry.*
He lifted me out of the slimy pit, out of the mud and mire;
he set my feet on a rock and gave me a firm place to stand.....

Praying for patience is like praying for rain, no one likes to wait and no one likes to get wet. Let patience have her perfect work so that ye may be perfect and mature, desiring nothing but God's best. During seasons of testing, waiting on God can be the hardest part. If you wait patiently on the Lord, he will hear your cry of distress and deliver you from the pit, and position you to stand victoriously in the face of adversity. God knows how to take you around the enemy and to keep you from unseen danger. Do not get ahead of God! Sometimes your deliverance is in the waiting. While you are waiting, God is working behind the scenes, to ensure your safety and release. Be free to wait on God knowing that He is the author and finisher of your faith. Jesus came that you might have life and life more abundantly. The righteous will never be forsaken. Though a host of painful situations may encamp against you, may your heart not fear; even if war arises against you, be confident in your waiting on the Lord. He shall lead and guide you beside the still waters.

Prayer

Hallelujah! Glory to the King of kings, and the Lord of lords. I will wait for you O' Lord, for you are my present help! I present my body as a living sacrifice holy and acceptable unto you, for it is my reasonable service. I will not get ahead of you Lord; I will wait faithfully upon you until you bring me out. I will run the race that has been set before me; I will leave those things which are behind. This season shall pass, and may I never forget your unfailing love towards me. Forgive me of my sins, and cleanse me from all unrighteousness. I choose to walk in agreement with your perfect will for my life. Lord, restore everything the locus has eaten, and bring light in the midst of darkness. My eyes are on you for you are my portion.

In Jesus Name,
Amen

Day 21

"Yet, Shall I Praise Him"

Psalm 42:5
Why are you downcast, O my soul? Why so disturbed within me? Put your hope in God, **for I will yet praise him**.....

There will be some days during a trying season in your life where you may not feel like getting out of the bed. The weight of the affliction, the unquenchable thirst for relief, and a feeling of being tired creeps in. On these days it takes more than your physical body getting out of the bed, but your soul must find relief and solace. The Psalmist understood these days, he also knew that although it felt like the weight of the world was upon his shoulders, there was a yet praise still available for his God. Today you may be contemplating what is the use of getting out of the bed, you may feel like you have lost and all odds are against you. Will you press past your present circumstances and put your hope in God? The enemy is betting against you today, he wants to see you give up and give in. Praise precedes breakthrough. Don't wait until you are on the other side of the storm to praise God, praise God now. Although you are not yet where you would like to be, there may not be a physical manifestation yet of what you have been hoping yet, praise God anyhow. Consider using your praise as a testimony of God's love and affection towards you. Use praise as a weapon against the forces of darkness that seek to overtake you in this season.

Praise unto the Lord breaks up the warfare and disarms the enemy. Praise says to your situation and circumstances that God is still good. The only thing standing between you and your breakthrough is a fresh perspective of who God is in your life. When you praise God in the midst of the storm, you exemplify true fellowship with his Spirit. Will you yet praise him?

Prayer

Lord, I thank you for turning my midnight into morning. I thank you for being a very present help in this season of trouble. You are my shield and my buckler, I will yet praise you! Let my life be a testimony to others that you are good and your mercy endures forever. Continue to protect my life from the enemy. I praise you for who you are my righteousness. I cast down every imagination and every high thing that would seek to exalt itself against the knowledge of Christ in my life. My life will not be the same after this season, because when I came into this season I had not yet fully known the power of your keeping power. I release my fears today, and I will allow my praise to reveal that you are yet good even in the storm. I trust you!

In Jesus Name,
Amen

Day 22

"I am the Lord's Servant"

Luke 1:38
***"I am the Lord's servant,"** Mary answered.*
"May it be to me as you have said"....

God knows what it will take to get you where he wants you to be. Stand still and see the salvation of the Lord. God knows your beginning and he sees your end, allow God to give you a fresh vision from Heaven. The mother of Jesus was given a glimpse of the Lord's will for her life. Her response was very important. How you respond in this season in your life will dictate how you end. If you respond with a negative posture and a slothful spirit, you could actually hinder yourself and others. Mary's response not only affected her life, but it affected many lives. Your response in this season in your life will be a demo of illustration to others. What are you modeling to others? Mary was resolved in the fact that she was the Lord's servant and that whatever the Lord was calling her to do or be, she was in total agreement. God may be asking you to do a hard thing today, he may be asking you to launch out into the deep. That launching out could be calling someone and asking for their forgiveness. God could be asking you to serve others in the midst of your pain. The word servant signifies that you have been called to service. All that you do in this life do it as unto the Lord. When God shows you or tells you what he wants you to do, remember that you are the Lord's servant. A servant does what his Master instructs.

Prayer

Jehovah Shalom,
I enter into your gates with thanksgiving today, I am thankful for your perfect will for my life. All that I am is because you loved me and preserved me during this season. My life is not my own, I freely choose to serve you and your people. As Mary stated Lord, I am your servant, let your will for my life be as you have said. I will no longer contend against what I don't understand, your love is amazing. You have loved me when I haven't loved myself. I give myself to you today, use me as you see fit. All for your glory!

In Jesus Name,
Amen

Day 23

"My Help comes From the Lord"

Psalm 121:1-2
I will lift up my eyes to the hills—
where does my help come from? My help comes from the LORD,
the Maker of heaven and earth......

During emergency situations many call 911 because of their ability to respond to crisis situations. When you call 911 you are often met with a voice on the other end asking where is the trouble. At that very moment the emergency assistance operator is working on your behalf to bring help to you. So it is in the spirit realm, when a child of God calls for help, Jesus Christ our Lord and Savior is moving on our behalf to bring help. That help might come in the form of divine intervention. God may have allowed the trouble to come in this season, so that he can show you that he is still available to you. Be careful not to miss how God will send help in the form of deliverance. God's ways are not our ways; his thoughts are not our thoughts. What seems impossible with men is very possible with God. If you are facing negative test results from the doctor and it looks like there is no hope, only embrace the fact that God is bigger than any circumstance or situation that you may be facing today. Remain faithful and obedient, lift up your eyes towards the hills from whence cometh your help, your help comes from God. If God chooses to use medical treatments opposed to supernatural healing be open. If God asks you to work through marital problems by submitting to the process instead of getting a divorce, be open. You may have to take a job for lesser pay than you are used to getting, God will provide all your needs according to his riches and glory. Look up, see his goodness, and receive his help. When you look up, you must also understand that he is looking down. God has a broader perspective of the situation, for he knows what's ahead. What hinders you in this season could actually be a blessing in the next. Receiving help from God will require that you do not lean on your own understanding, but acknowledge him and he shall direct your path.

Prayer

***O' Majestic One, Holy One of Israel,
I sit at your feet today, and I open up my alabaster box and pour out my love and affection upon you. I look up to see the beauty of your continence and how you are smiling upon me today, because I am calling out to you for help. Help me to not try to fix myself or others today. Help me to embrace spiritual truth and not worldly efforts. My heart is open to you and I pray that you would heal me. Help me to see my life as you see it, a gift and not a disaster. I will be courageous, I will not shrink back for you will not have any pleasure in me. Help me to learn the beauty of contentment, for I will be content in whatever season I find myself in because you have helped***

me to see that it is not all about me, but about fulfilling your will for my life.

In Jesus Name,
Amen

Day 24

"Rejoice in our Sufferings"

Romans 5: 3-5
***Rejoice in our sufferings**, because we know that suffering produces perseverance;*
Perseverance, character; and character, hope.....

There are some surgeries that are elective, and there are some that are mandatory. During seasons of change, you may experience spiritual surgery. This surgery takes place on the inside of our spirits, minds and hearts. God desires to give you a new spirit and a new heart. In the natural when someone has heart problems, surgery is often necessary to fix faulty arteries or to bring a healthy flow of blood into the heart. In this season, God may be working on your heart. This work may not be as you know it to be, a new heart may be required spiritually so that you can love more. Your spiritual arteries may be blocked by past hurts and past pain that are literally preventing you from loving as God has commanded you to love. The lack of love flowing from your heart may be stopping you from fulfilling your purpose in the earth. God wants to take away your stony heart and replace it with one that is fleshy. It will take the love of God flowing through you to help you be effective in ministering to His people. This surgery is not elective it is mandatory for the believer to reflect Christ in the earth. Any type of surgery will bring some suffering. Surgery whether natural or spiritual is painful in many ways, and the healing process can produce suffering from the effects of the surgery and it is necessary. Don't abort this part of the process. Rejoice in your suffering, this type of suffering will produce perseverance and godly character so that you will be complete and lacking nothing. A new spirit requires a mindset change, and a dying to self. If we suffer with Christ we will also be raised with him. The new spirit is the Spirit of Christ dwelling in you to effectually bring you into a state of kingdom mindset. Suffer for a moment and rejoice for a lifetime.

Prayer

My God whom I love,
I submit to the surgery that must take place in my heart today. You are free to uproot deeply seated past pains and hurts within my heart. Father I trust you to use everything the enemy attempted to use for evil, to turn it around for my good. I release every person that has hurt me. I willingly forgive my offenders and the offenses, please forgive me. I pray that you will help me to love as you have commanded me. I shall rejoice in my sufferings because I know that my end shall be greater than my beginning. Restore my joy, remove the pain, I trust in your name Jesus and the latter rain. Make me over into who you would have me to be!

In Jesus Name,
Amen

Day 25

"Pray for the Comforter"

John 14:16
I will pray to the Father, and he shall give you another Comforter,
that he may abide with you.....

This is not the season to be abstract in your thinking. You may be rehearsing over and over in your mind about what you are going through, and why are you going through this. It is time to rely on the Father and the one He has promised to send to you when you are in need. Pray today out of your spirit and not your intellect. The presence of God in the midst of a turbulent season can make the very difference on whether or not you remain sane and in your right mind. Pray to your Heavenly Father today; ask him to send the Comforter which is the Holy Spirit. The Spirit knows what to pray even when you don't, He will search the deep things of God and make intercession through you. Be available today to receive the gift that the Lord wants to give you. Human reasoning goes out the window when He comes, carnal thinking and pity parties will soon dissipate. No longer will you need to strive, only abide with Him. Today will be a day of release for you as you begin down the journey of wisdom, revelation and renewal. When the Spirit of Truth comes, he will not speak of His own, but only what He hears the Father say. The Comforter will bring light to a dark situation, clarity of mind to a once tormented and distressful state. Begin to build an altar right where you are. This is the place where you will lie down your burdens, and lift up Holy adoration to the one who loves you more than your circumstances. Ask God for a renewed sense of His presence in your life. Resist the devil today and he will flee. God desires to take you on a journey today to the high places in Him, pray and ask for the Comforter.

Prayer

Holy Spirit Come, Spirit of Truth you are welcome, I desire truth in my inner being today. Expose all the lies and deceits in my thinking today bring forth a renewed sense of truth and clarity. I effectually receive the leading of the Spirit of God. I need your help today be my Helper. I pray for the Comforter today, to meet me in those places in me that are unsure and vulnerable. I am your sheep Lord, and I know your voice. Speak Lord by your Spirit, and the voice of a stranger I shall not follow. I reject the way that seems right, and all of its false appearances. I choose Jesus today, because He is the truth, the way, and the light. I come to the Father today to be comforted in my soul, in my mind, and in my heart. Release the healing balm today to comfort my sorrowful and weary soul.

In Jesus Name,
Amen

Day 26
"Cast Down Imaginations"

2 Cor. 10:5
Casting down imaginations, *and every high thing that exalts itself against the knowledge of God, and bringing into captivity every thought to the obedience of Christ......*

While growing up many of us were taught religious rituals and a false sense of knowledge concerning who God is. Maybe you were fortunate enough to avoid this type of unhealthy impartation, whichever side you came from; there will come a time in your life where you will need to know God for yourself. What is your image of God in your life today? Is there anything preventing you from seeing him as all-sufficient? There are seasons that will come in your life where you might feel that God has abandoned you, that God doesn't care enough about you to instantly deliver you from a situation. When these types of accusations come to your mind, you will need to begin to cast down imaginations. These imaginations can look like your worst nightmare coming true, or maybe a thought that rises to say that God and the world is against you. God will reveal to you what areas of your life that needs to be brought into captivity to the obedience of Christ. Hear and obey! Trust the process of gaining a renewed mind. Pause and begin to thank God for the illumination that is taking place in your thought life today. If you allow faulty thinking to govern you, you willingly give yourself over to defeat. Begin to think and set your mind on those things that are good and the peace of God will guard and protect your heart and your mind. The battlefield of the mind is where victory or defeat is decided.

Prayer

Elohim, El shaddi,
You are my rock and my salvation, in you do I trust. I repent for any carnal thinking that did not please you. I have the mind of Christ! I will not accept the lies of the enemy today. I will cast down every imagination that seeks to exalt itself against the knowledge of Christ in my life. The battle is not mine, but it is yours Lord. I will hear and obey. Position me to receive truth today and reject all lies of the deceitful one. I will be transformed today by the renewing of my mind. It is in you that I live move and have my being. It is so!

In Jesus Name,
Amen

Day 27
"Pray That Your Faith Not Fail"

Luke 22: 31-32
Satan has asked to sift you as wheat. ***But I have prayed for you, that your faith may not fail****. And when you have turned back, strengthen your others......*

Take a deep breath. As you inhale the Lord's love exhale any emotions that have tried to wear you down. The Lord's love will begin to fill those areas of damaged emotions that have tried to cause you pain at some point in your life. Damaged emotions are like leaky valves in the human heart. This can cause the heart to become faulty and fragile. In fact, if the issue is not addressed and fixed, the lack of blood flow to the heart can become deadly. They cause the disruption of the love of God from being free to move in your life. God wants to stop the leak; God wants to remove the pain. The enemy of your soul has desired to sift you as wheat. This means that he wants to take advantage of your weakened state. He knows the areas in which you have been hurt and disappointed. God's love can cover a multitude of sin. Make a confession of faith today that you will not give up or into this season of stress and disappointment. Trust in the Lord's ability to bring you forth as pure gold. Jesus is praying for you during this season in your life that your faith fails not, and once you received your deliverance you be prepared and willing to help others. Look back over your life for a moment; acknowledge that it is God who has kept you thus far. The same keeping power is available now for you. Your Heavenly Father loves you and he knows what you need, without faith it is impossible to please God.

Prayer

O' Holy One of Israel,
I sit at your feet today. I bask in your presence. I am a child of the Most High God; I will wait to hear what you will say to me today. I know that without faith it is impossible to please you! You are attentive to the prayers of those that are yours, for that I am so thankful.
I declare that I shall not fall or faint in this season of testing and trials. Greater is He that is in me than he that is in this world. I will take heart, I will be of good cheer, for you said that in this life I would have tribulations, I will stay in peace for you have overcome the world!

In Jesus Name,
Amen

Day 28
"God Has not Given you a Spirit of Fear"

2 Timothy 1:7
For God hath not given us the spirit of fear*; but of power, and of love, and of a sound mind.*

It is very hard to drive a car through a dark road especially when a storm has just hit. The car may have started to slip and slide, and you feel like it's a struggle to keep control of the car. You are not sure what's ahead in the road, the possibility of hitting or running into something can cause such a fear. This is what dark seasons in life can look and feel like. You have just been hit with some unexpected news or event, your world starts spinning out of control at least that is what it feels like. You are struggling to keep control of everything around you, yet fear of what you might have to face ahead has crept in. You will need to know that God has not giving you a spirit of fear, but he has given you power, and His love, so that your mind can be at peace. One thing about storms they do lift. God desires to take you through the storm with the abilities that only he can give you to sustain in the midst of uncertainty. Giving your life to God, means giving him control. Fear immobilizes, it demoralizes the impact of your position in God. Stand, having done all to do stand! Once God reveals himself to you in the storm, keep that image before you. He is with you; he will never leave you nor forsake you. You may have played a part in the storm coming; you may have given way to the fear. Fear not, for God neither sleeps nor slumbers, as he watches over Israel he is watching over you. Nothing can separate you from His love. God desires fellowship in the inward parts, commune with him spirit to spirit today. For those who worship Him must worship Him in spirit and in truth. Where truth is present fear cannot prevail!

Prayer

God Almighty,

I adore you today, I acknowledge your holiness and I bless your name! You know what's ahead; I give you total control today. I yield to the name that is above all names. My Redeemer Lives and I have hope in my redemption and restoration. Though, this season has come to sleigh me yet shall I trust you! You have not given me the spirit of fear; I reject all forms of fear today. I receive the power and the love that has been made available to me through Jesus. Lord, take my mind today for it is sound in you. I rebuke fear, doubt and unbelief from having any place in my life. I come to the foot of the cross, for His (Jesus) death paid it all. I can go on to fight this fight of faith because He rose with all power and might in His hand! The war in my mind IS FINISHED, my faith shall prevail in this season!

In Jesus Name,
Amen

Day 29
"Pray for the Pillar"

Exodus 13:21
By day the LORD went ahead of them in a ***pillar of cloud***
to guide them on their way
and by night in a ***pillar of fire*** *to give them light......*

When a caterpillar is ready to become a butterfly, there is an inner struggle that takes place. There is transformation that is taking place in the midst of the struggle. It is however oblivious to the caterpillar at the time of metamorphism because of its present state of distress. This reflects those who are experiencing an inner struggle to become and be who God is calling them to be. What are you struggling with today? It is said that if the caterpillar's process of becoming a butterfly is interrupted, the process could be aborted and the caterpillar could miss the opportunity for growth. You may find yourself in a somewhat uncomfortable position today, pray for the pillar. God is your pillar, your strength and present help; He will go before you to provide guidance as you are transformed into the image of His Son Jesus. The struggle you are feeling should be eased by knowing that at your darkest times God will shed light so that you are not given over to destruction. You will not walk in condemnation or fear that often accompany the night, nor the lies of the enemy that may come today. Many of your present day challenges will fall by the way as you uphold the word of the Lord today, and many more will fall as you continue to trust

God along this journey into the high places of God. Press through the pain today of thinking you need to have it all together, God has it all together and He delights in you.

Prayer

God,
Help me with my struggles today. Help me not to abort the process of becoming who you are calling me to be. You are my strength, you are my pillar. I lean not on my own understanding, but I am acknowledging you today in all of my ways. Help me to see that I don't need to have it all together in this process, but as I continue to trust you I understand that I need you more today than I did on yesterday. Guide me through this season, go before me Father. It is amazing grace that has saved a wretch like me, and it will be your unfailing love to deliver me. Lord, I am uncomfortable, but I understand that this is a necessary part of my transformation. Take delight today Lord in what you see, get the glory out of my life according to your perfect will.
In Jesus Name,
Amen

Day 30
"In Due Season"

Galatians 6:9
And let us not be weary in well doing: ***for in due season*** *we shall reap, if we faint not.*

Waiting for change is a precursor to being ready for the new season ahead. Those who wait upon the Lord he shall renew their strength. It can be likened to waiting upon the mail carrier to deliver an expected package to your house. You have the guarantee from the shipper that the shipment will take place, but you have to wait until the scheduled time. If you are looking for the package to come at 3 o'clock but it is not due until 5 o'clock then your waiting will be in vain. Do not let your labor in this season be in vain. Do not grow weary in your waiting on God, for in his appointed timing, in due season you shall be rewarded for your faithfulness if you do not give up. Many have waxed cold and have chosen rather to curse God and die. Ask God to cleanse you with hyssop which is his anointing so that you will be fortified and sustained. The race is not given to those that want to rush the process that God has them in, but to those who endure and hold out hope until the end. Press towards the mark of his high calling upon your life. The press is meant to bring you to a place of total dependence on God in this season. Refuse to accept defeat and discouragement. These will only become bonds of yoke placed around your neck by the evil one. Reclaim your freedom today, mount up wings like an eagle. You shall run and not grow weary, you shall walk and not faint. God is watching over his word to perform it. For in due season, you shall reap a harvest.

Prayer

El Shaddai,

You are the God of the Universe; you created me I am your workmanship created in Christ Jesus. I rejoice in the God of my Salvation! It is appointed once unto man to die, than you will judge our works. You have appointed the times and nothing is hidden from you! I choose to depend on you in this season. You have appointed how long this season in my life should last; help me not to prolong it with murmuring and complaining. In due season, I shall come forth as pure gold, help me not to watch the clock, but to watch you! I refuse to accept defeat or discouragement, cleanse me with hyssop today; I confess my sins, wash me and cleanse me of all unrighteousness. I am the Beloved of God!

In Jesus Name,
Amen

Day 31
"Find Joy in His Presence"

Psalm 16:11
You have made known to me the path of life; ***you will fill me with joy in your presence****......*

The mile markers on the freeway help you to know how many miles you have traveled, and they let you know where you are in position to your destination. When the mile marker signifies that you are nearing your destination, there is a sense of relief and joy that comes. This comes from a sense of accomplishment of how far one has traveled. Take a spiritual survey of the road you have been traveling on. The straight and narrow path leads to life, the broad and the wide path leads to more pain and disappointment, many chose this one. Choose the road less traveled and recognize that God has made known to you the path of life, so that you will be filled with the joy of knowing his presence. The presence of God can be your mile marker as to which path you have chosen. If you do not have the joy of His presence accompanying you today, you missed the mile marker that signified his grace and mercy that was made available to you. When you have joy, you understand that the joy of the Lord is your strength. The presence of God speaks of your ability to remain in him while you are on this journey; the joy is the fruit that is born as a result of staying on the path of life. If you have missed your exit make a shift today and repent and return unto the Lord. Restoration is always available for the believer. When you pass through the waters of life they will not overtake you, when you have to endure fiery trials you shall not be consumed! For the Lord your God will save you and deliver you from this momentary affliction. Ask the Lord to restore your joy today and remove the pain, trust in His word as he brings the latter rain. Your latter shall be greater than your former, stay on the path of life.

Prayer

Master,
How I long to be in your presence. One thing I desire today, that is to dwell in the presence of the Lord all the days of my life, and to behold your beauty. I drink of the cup that you have given me today! I present my body a living sacrifice holy and acceptable unto you today. I desire the joy that comes from being in your presence. The joy of the Lord is my strength. Restore my joy today and remove the pain of the past and the present. Weeping may endure for a season, but I declare joy shall come. Lord, you are the vine, and I am the branch, may I bear the fruit of joy by staying connected to you through this season. I shall live and not die. My later seasons shall be greater than past seasons. In your presence is fullness of joy!

In Jesus Name,
Amen

Day 32
"I Exalt Thee Oh Lord"

Isaiah 25: 1
O LORD, you are my God; ***I will exalt you and praise your name****,*
for in perfect faithfulness you have done marvelous things,
things planned long ago.

Praise God for every victory that he has given you in this season. Attribute all honor and glory to him. When the President of the United Sates enters into an army base, the soldiers immediately salute him giving honor to the office that he holds. When the King of Kings enters into your life, you must honor him as Commander and Chief. You are a soldier on the battle field of the Lord. As an earthly commander gives commands and issues directives, so it is in the Heavenly realm. God has given you a command in which you are to govern your life by and that is, thou shall love the Lord thy God with all of your heart, mind and soul. Praise is comely for the upright. Exalt God today and praise his Holy name for he is worthy of all of your praise. Your praise unto God disarms the attack of depression, self-pity, and loneliness. Praise the Lord in the beauty of holiness. Put on your garments of praise today! Shout unto the Lord with a voice of triumph. Make a list of things to praise God for today, set your affection upon him. Love on God today and give him the praise that is due his name. Great is the Lord and greatly to be praised. Lift up your head today with exalted praise that the King of Glory might come in! Your current situation will need to take a back seat when you give God the front seat of your focus. Begin to center your attention towards him, bring glory to him for his perfect faithfulness and the marvelous things that he has done.

Prayer

My Lord, My King,
You are worthy to be praised, from the rising of the sun to the going down of the same, you alone are worthy. I esteem you high today; my act of worship and praise is because before I was you were. I exalt you and give your name the praise that is due. I praise you for all that you do and will do in my life in this season. I will not be moved by what my situation looks like, you have the final word, and I trust in you. I cast off all restraints of stress, anxiety, and worry today and I will dance before you. I shout with a voice of victory and expectation. Make my enemies a lie and take full authority in your position as King of my life! The devil is under my feet, he is a defeated foe. I praise you in advance, for praise is comely for the upright.

In Jesus Name,
Amen

Day 33
"Pray for the Renewing of Your Mind"

Romans 12:2

Be ye transformed by the renewing of your mind, that ye may prove what is that good, and acceptable, and perfect, will of God.....

What appears intangible becomes tangible when you begin to renew your mind. What seems out of reach then becomes within reach. The wall of protection begins to dispute the pain of rejection, a false sense of self, and a disturbed conscious. The prelude to transformation is birthed out of a fresh sense of mind over matter. In this season you will need to prove that which is good, and acceptable perfect will of God. The proof comes in the form of being able to discern evil from good. Make a mental decision today to regain spiritual consciousness and an acute form of connection to your eternal source. When positive thoughts begin to overcome a reprobate mindset, victory is assured. Prove today that which is good. God is good and His mercy endures forever. The will of God is that you flourish. You will be like the tree that is planted by the rivers of living water that in its ordained season of newness will flourish and will not fall. A righteous person falls seven times but they get back up. The fall could represent a sense of failure, but know that your Redeemer lives and He lives to restore you. Take this time of preparation to build your relationship with God. The preparation creates the way for transformation. The atmosphere of a season changing causes one to remember the seeds that were sowed in a previous season. If you will sow into this season in your life seeds of trust, faith, and obedience, you will reap a harvest of joy, peace, and love in the season to come. Submit those areas in your mind today that need to be renewed unto God, allow him to prove to you which are good and acceptable. Let His will be done!

Prayer

Hallelujah to the One who sits high and looks low. Thank you Lord for regarding my low estate today, you are my Savior! Save me today from every evil thought of self-destruction. I pray for the renewing of my mind today. I declare my transformation from the inside out. Make me over into who you would have me to be. I make a conscious decision to stay connected to you today. May I make every effort to seek your counsel in every decision that needs to be made today? Give me discernment and wisdom in this season. Lord, prove through me that which is your good and acceptable will for my life.

In Jesus Name,
Amen

Day 34
"Submit to God and Resist the Devil"

James 4:7
Submit yourselves therefore to God. Resist the devil,
and he will flee from you……

There are certain exercises that can be done to help build resistance in the muscles. This resistance is to help the body be able to maintain stamina and endurance. Have you built up your spiritual stamina and endurance? How are you resisting the devil today? Can you endure this season of testing? Submit unto God always and then you will be able to resist the devil and his schemes. The staying power that you need will come from your ability to submit to your Heavenly Father. How well you endure under adverse circumstances is connected to God's ability to take you under his wings, He will save you from the fowler's trap. God will not have you ignorant of the devices of the devil. You must exercise your kingdom power and authority over every situation in your life today. God has given you power to trample over the scorpions and the power of the evil one, and nothing by any means shall harm you. Submission to God means taking him by his word. He is not a man that he should lie, nor the son of man that he should repent, your God has decreed no weapon that is forged against you shall prosper. Give the enemy no ground to stand on, take the floor from up under him. Keep submitting your life unto God; continue to call on the name of Jesus. This act of worship unto God will emancipate the darkness that would try to overtake you. Do not be ritualistic at this time; be intentional about disarming and dismantling anything that would try to have you bound today. Resist the devil and he will flee.

Prayer

Heavenly Father, My Righteousness,
You paid the cost, for the penalty for sin is eternal death.
Without you, I would be doomed to eternal damnation.
I will resist the devil today and he will flee. I submit all areas of my life to you today including the areas that I am struggling with. My momentary affliction does not have a lasting impact on your ability to move mountains on my behalf. Where can I go from your presence? I did not choose you, but you chose me. Thank you Father for preserving my life from the evil one, I declare Satan has no hold on my life, all of his tactics will fall to naught.
Uphold me in this season, give me assurance of my victory, I will submit my ways to you first, and resist the ways of the devil and he will flee,
I degree it to be so and it shall be.

In Jesus Name,
Amen

Day 35
"Meditate on His Word Day and Night"

Joshua 1:8
Do not let this Book of the Law depart from your mouth;
meditate on it day and night,
Then you will be prosperous and successful…….

Shadowing those who went before you in the faith can provide that encouragement that you need to survive adversity and unfavorable seasons in your life. Witnessing God's provision and protection in the lives of others can provide an outline for you. God's word is instructional and beneficial. When you need direction for your life, seek the wisdom that comes from reading God's word. Seek Him while He may be found. Mediate on His word day and night, so that you will be prosperous and victorious. That mediation should take place in the day which represents the good seasons and the night representing the challenging seasons. God's word offers a host of biblical examples of those who were challenged in their lives and how God brought them out. You have not because you ask not. Ask and it shall be given unto you. Ask God to show you the ancient paths, the paths that are proven, the way that he led others out of the wilderness. Trust God to respond, and when he does, hear and obey. Do not let his word of instruction depart from you. Hold fast to the profession of your faith. Ask God to ignite the fire within you to consume his word continually. As the Lord pours into you, you will be able to pour into others once you have overcome. God wants you to be prosperous and successful because he loves you. Meditation on God's word takes your mind off of your current situation and places your focus on Him, who is bigger than your situation. Vegetables need light and water to grow. You need the light of God's word and the saturation of His Spirit to grow in this season. Without either you will wither and grow faint and that is not the will of the Father for your life. Extreme makeover is required in this season; God may have you revisit some broken areas in your life so that you can begin to experience freedom and stop being victimized by your past experiences. Then he will make your way blessed.

Prayer

Abba Father,
My Rock, in whom I do trust in this season of my life my soul, doth magnify the Lord! I will meditate on your word day and night. Send a refreshing today; water every dry area in my life. Help me to embrace this season of change. May I see my reflection in your word. I seek you early while you may be found. Make my way prosperous in this season of my life. I will not let your book of the law depart from my mouth. Father, saturate me with the very essence of your presence. Visit me and reveal yourself more and more to me. Help me to see those things that have been hidden from me. Expose the traps of the evil one so that I do not dash my foot against a stone. I agree

with your word, it is true and you are not a man that you should lie. Your word will I meditate on day and night!

In Jesus Name,
Amen

Day 36
"Pray for the Peace of God"

Philippians 4: 7
The peace of God, which passeth all understanding,
shall keep your hearts and minds through Christ Jesus.

When an ordeal surfaces and the effects are both troublesome and tiresome, you will desire some form of relief. Pray for the peace of God. The beginning of a thing does not dictate the end of the matter. No matter what it looks like today; gloomy, uncertain, hopeless, the peace of God will keep your heart and your mind through Christ Jesus. Do not allow the present conditions to become a stumbling block. God wants to send a fresh wave of His peace your way. Often times there are organizations that provide a form of relief aid to those who are hungry and homeless. Their main objective is to meet the present need. God desires to meet you right where you are, in the midst of this season. The peace of God will come and surpass all your understanding, pray and ask God to send the peace. The peace of God will still the troubled waters and silence the taunting voice of the enemy. There is safety in the peace of God. Peace is a benefit of His presence being available in your life. God's peace is more than a concept to be understood, it is a benefit of being an heir to the throne of God. Mercy and justice belong to the Father. He knows how to give good gifts to His children. Prayer says that you will accept the gift that has been made available to you. Remain humble and obedient. The season of testing will passover you, you must ensure that the blood of Jesus is on the doorpost of your heart. When this season passes over you will be left still standing, it will not be in your own strength but in the one who created you. Pray for the peace of God to keep you today.

Prayer

Jehovah Shalom,
I love and adore you today. I repent for any action or mindset that has become a stumbling block to me receiving your peace. I want the peace that only you can give and not what the world has to offer. I am praying for a fresh wave of your anointing of peace and tranquility. In the midst of this season, I choose to take refuge in your peace. I do not understand all that I must go through, but your peace will surpass all my understanding and strengthen my heart and my mind in Christ Jesus. I declare peace be still in every area of my life today. The blood of Jesus is against you Satan; you have no power and no authority in my life. I am the righteousness of God! You are my peace today Lord and I trust you, all things are working together for my good because I am called according to your purpose in this season.

In Jesus Name,
Amen

Day 37
"Pick up Your Cross"

Mark 8:34
He said unto them; whosoever will come after me, let him deny himself, and ***take up his cross, and follow me.***

Following someone takes effort and humility. Adjustments will need to be made so that as you follow you will remain at a close distance to that of the one leading so you are not led astray. There are some drawbacks to following someone; you will not be the one making the decisions, and you will be impacted by the direction they lead you in. You will have to sacrifice your independence and you will need to work on your attitude. So, it is when you decide to follow after Jesus Christ. Those that follow after Christ must deny themselves and must give up their dependence on self. There will need to be a total denial of selfishness because it could be a deterrent in the destination that He wants to lead you in. There is a cost to following after Christ. The cost is likened to the cross of Christ. During this season, you may have to sacrifice a moment of pleasure for a lifetime of blessings. It is a two part process to following the Savior; the first part precedes the second. The first part speaks to self- denial which leads to rejecting idolatry and self gratification these are the initial steps that lead into the second step of the self-disciplined life of the disciple. Only in this can one truly follow Christ. It is not in the knowing, it is in the doing. Your response in this season requires that you come to Christ and lay down your life of self as you know it and accept the life that God wants to give you. For God is the author and the finisher of your faith. A life lived unto self is not a God given life. Pick up your cross today and follow after him.

Prayer

My Father which art in Heaven hollowed by thy name, they Kingdom Come they will be done in my life today. Today I count the cost of following you. I willingly lose my independence for total dependence upon you. I deny myself and all selfish ambitions today. My life is not my own, my live belongs to you O' God. I pick up my cross and I follow after you. I want to know you more and the power of your might. Help me to adjust those things that would prevent me from fully following after you. I want to pass this test. I want the light of your Spirit in my life to shine in the midst of darkness. Awaken those things within me that need to come alive to the things of God. Help me to know and embrace that you require a broken spirit and a contrite heart. My cross Lord will I pickup and follow after you!

In Jesus Name,
Amen

Day 38
"With God all things are Possible"

Matthew 19:26
But Jesus beheld them, and said unto them,
With men this is impossible;
***but with God all things are possible*.**

The headlines on the newspaper proclaim that there is no hope of the world turning around. Man's predictions are often filled with a lack of hope and impossibilities. If we are not careful we will believe the report of the world. Whose report will you believe today? Does it appear that this season in your life will last always? Does the doctor's report speak of indefinites and the inability to provide you with a good prognosis? Does your marriage look like it's beyond repair, and divorce is inevitable? You haven't heard from your child and you are not sure if they will ever accept Christ in their lives? Renounce any evidence of a lack of faith in your God. Repent and turn your ears back to the one who holds your very future in the palm of His hand. With men these things are impossible, but with God all things are possible. Use the word of God as your plumb line, measure the impossibilities up against God's word of possibilities. There have been many false predictions since the beginning of the church as to when Christ would return. No man knows the hour or the season, so it is in your life. Allow no one to speak uncertainties of death and destruction over your life. Let hope spring alive in you and nurture your God given right to call those things that be not as though they are. Sincerity accompanied by a child like faith brings a God like blessing into your life. Be open to receive what God has for you today. Approach the throne of grace with boldness and confidence. Do not throw away your confidence which has a great recompense of reward. With God all things are possible.

Prayer

Almighty and Awesome God,
I bow to thee this day, your greatness is beyond words. You are the air that I breathe today. My hope and my future is in your hands. I do not care what it looks like today, if you speak one word then my situation will change. I know and understand that with you God all things are possible. My life belongs to you and I yield and surrender all unto you this day. Take my mind and mold it, take my life and control it. I will not throw away my confidence which has great recompense of reward, for when I have done the will of God and done all that I know how to do, I will stand! I choose to belief your report, I have the victory in Christ Jesus.

In Jesus Name,
Amen

Day 39
"Be His Witness"

Acts 22:15
For thou shalt ***be his witness*** *unto all men of what thou hast seen and heard........*

In the court of law, there may be witnesses called to testify in regards to the litigations that may need to be supported or refuted. Witnesses are important, because they shed light on the actual events that are being either disputed or supported. In some cases no witness can determine the fate of a case. God is calling you to be a witness today. Someone needs to hear how God is keeping you in this season of transformation. You will need to testify that God exists in the valley as well as on the mountaintop. It is important that you testify that God is a God of relationship. He doesn't just send help; He actually comes to be the help you need so that you can overcome. Be His witness today unto all that He may lead on your path, testify of what he has shown you and told you. Testifying before others may not be easy; it will cause you to be transparent and vulnerable. You may have to share the ugliness of a situation to show the beauty of God's amazing grace. All of the details are significant, for you do not know which part of your testimony will strengthen and encourage the next. Many will overcome by the word of your testimony and by the shed blood of Christ. Be encouraged to share your faith with others today. Will you be a witness for God? Do not hide the light of your testimony up under a bushel, but tell your story so that others will see your progress and glorify your Father in Heaven. Your story may be the very encouragement that someone else needs to break forth this season. Go and tell it on the mountain, at school, at work, at church, etc., that Jesus Christ lives and that he lives in you!

Prayer

Eternal Father,
I bless your name today. I am your witness today of your steadfast love. I will testify of the goodness of the Lord. You are just and you are faithful. It does rain on the just and the unjust. I am a written epistle for all men to read. Use me today as your vessel of honor unto your throne. My story of hope and redemption is meant to strengthen others. Lord lead others along the path today so that I may tell of your mercy, for it endures forever. There is nothing to hard for you, and you are not slack in your promises. I will overcome by the blood of the lamb and by the word of my testimony. Jesus lives, and because he lives I shall live and not die. I accept the great commission today; I will go and be your disciple today because I love you and want to serve you and your kingdom.

In Jesus Name,
Amen

Day 40
"For a Season"

Luke 4:13
And when the devil had ended all the temptation, he departed from him ***for a season****.*

There is indeed a time for everything and a season for every action this side of heaven. God makes everything beautiful in His time. He has set eternity in the hearts of those who are His. Everything that God does will endure forever, no one can take away from you what you have learned in this season. It is a gift from God. It is written, "That man shall not live by bread alone, but by every word that precedes out of the mouth of God." Weeping and times of testing may endure for a season but then comes joy, freedom, endurance, resistance, peace, love, grace, and transformation coupled with a newness for life. The testing of your faith in this season should have brought forth perseverance. This season came that you will be completely mature in him, lacking nothing. Blessed you will be when you persevere in a trying season in your life, because when you have stood the test, you shall receive the crown of life from God as He has promised you. Judge not your brother or your sister who may be entering a season of testing, or you will be judged. Remain faithful and obedient. Continue to feed upon His word, meditate on it day and night, so that he will make your way prosperous and successful. He alone knows the way that you must go and after the testing comes the purification. When an evil affliction leaves a person, it will go searching for a place of rest, it will try to return. Do not allow the evil one to find your house empty of God's love towards Him and His people. The accuser of your soul will try to return and bring more havoc into your life. For when the devil has ended all of his attacks and accusations against you during this season of trials in your life, he will only depart for a season. Keep God's word in your mouth and remember God's unfailing love towards you. You have the victory in Christ Jesus!

Prayer

Lord of the Breakthrough,
I declare your glory in the earth today! You are the great I AM, you are the God that is more than enough. You have kept me with your mighty hand, and your outstretched arm during this season. As I emerge from this season of testing and tribulation, may I never forget that it was you who led me these 40 days. Thank you for humbling me, and testing me to know what was in my heart. I know now that I do not live by bread alone, but by every word that comes from you O' Lord! I will keep your commands, I will help strengthen others. My mind has been renewed, and I have experienced transformation. I will remain faithful and obedient. There is joy in your presence. I pray for the continued presence of the Comforter. Holy Spirit fill me up, for I know the enemy of my soul will return after a season, but he will not find me

devoid of your Spirit. Greater is He that is in me, than he that is in this world.

In Jesus Name,
Amen

Reflection

After you have come through a season of testing and trials you must reflect on the journey. There are some lessons learned during ***A Season of Prayer*** that must remain a part of your spiritual artillery. God has equipped you for future battles so now there should be a longing in your spirit to help someone else. There are some lifetime decisions made that must be reflected upon. How did God reveal himself to you, and how did you respond? Your perspective looking back should be different than when you began this journey. There is only one true way to know if your journey was not in vain. If your passion and zeal for God is greater than when you began, you're coming out is a sign of your faith and your commitment to godliness and service. How have you adjusted to your new season? If your faith in the God who sees you has grown, you should have on a garment of praise. If your light is shining brighter than the darkness that once tried to cover your life, God has given you beauty for ashes. If your compassion for others is genuine, your mourning has been turned into joy. Your prayer life now should reflect a more intimate relationship with your Heavenly Father. You should know him and cry out to him as Abba Father. The law of reciprocity is biblical. The dedication and commitment that you have sowed into this **Season of Prayer** shall surely reap a harvest. When you drink of the living water, you will never thirst again. This doesn't mean you will not be challenged again, this doesn't mean that you won't face pain again. But it means that you know that your Heavenly Father is there for you and with you. It is my heart's desire and the intent behind writing this devotional **A Season of Prayer 40 Day Devotional for Women**, is that each day you connected with God in devotion and in prayer. If you are reading this devotional I believe God orchestrated this divine connection. I pray that my journey has inspired and encouraged you on to greater works in Him.

Be Blessed!

Reflection Questions

1. What was the most valuable truth you learned this season?

2. How has your relationship with God changed?

3. What has God required for you to give up during this season?

4. What have you learned about how you handle difficult seasons, what would you change?

5. Can you see God more clearly operating in your life?

6. Are you the same person that you were before you went on this journey?

7. Will you share your journey with the intent of helping others?

8. **Have you begun to see the beauty in the testing? If not, why?**

9. **What is the path that God is leading you to now?**

10. **How important is repentance in your life now than before starting this journey?**

Notes

Notes

Notes

Notes

Notes

LaVergne, TN USA
07 August 2010
192362LV00003B/3/P

9 781609 572075